Bow Down

Bow Down

Rough Raw & Ready

Chavanese Wint

Published by Icons Media Publishing in 2024

Copyright © Chavanese Wint

First Edition

The author asserts the moral right under the Copyright, Designs and Patents Act 1988 to be identified as the author of this work.

All Rights reserved. No part of this publication may be reproduced, stored in a retrieval system or transmitted, in any form or by any means without the prior consent of the author, nor be otherwise circulated in any form of binding or cover other than that in which it is published and without a similar condition being imposed on the subsequent purchaser.

Table of Contents

Healthy Eating *1*
Basic Nutrition *3*
Dawn's Delight *5*
Next-Door Chronicles *6*
Enigma *7*
Rough Waters *9*
Sex Symbol *11*
Forbidden Temptations *13*
Oral Delight *14*
Rough, Raw & Ready *15*
Libido Boost *16*
Neutral Territory *17*
The Art of Learning *19*
Nourish & Thrive *21*
Big Fat Extravaganza *22*
Excitement *23*
Art of Romancing *24*
Jackpot Dick *25*
Bruised & Amused *27*
Less is More *28*
Art That Strips *30*
Sex Life Unfiltered *31*
Sex Past Thirty *32*
Sex Preparation *33*
Sex Obsession *35*
Through the Cracks *37*
Sex Date *39*

CRAVING	41
Sex Potion	42
Melodies of Desire	44
The Art of Exhibitionism	45
The Pleasure Palace	47
Playing for Pleasure	48
From Foreplay to Finale	50
Big Dirty Dick's Diary	52
Sex Power	53
Forbidden Desires	55
Pussy Riot	57
Mind Games	59
Sex Reward	61
Awakened	62
Carnal Connections	64
Sensual Canvas	66
Possessed by You	67
Horny Horizons	69
Fatal Lust	71
The Sex Clutch Chronicles	73
Sexvation	74
The Orgasmic Cure for Stress	76
Hunger for Healing	78
Orgasmic Odyssey	80

DEDICATION

I dedicate this book to you, not only for the reasons why you wicked up its pages and ordered it, but also for your desire to explore the depths of a fearless writer's mind. This captivating book, titled "Bow Down Rough Raw and Ready," is a testament to your engagement with art and literature. With every word penned on these pages, I aim to enthrall you with the power of language and the raw beauty of the human body. From the dedication page to the final chapter, this book is an invitation to delve into a world where boundaries are pushed, where passion reigns supreme. So let us embark on this journey together, where oral and anal expressions intertwine with poetic elegance, where the pulsating rhythm of desire echoes through each sentence. This book is dedicated to you - my reader, my muse - for your unwavering support and for embracing the rough, raw, and ready nature of artistic expression.

To Shermaine Campbell

Healthy Eating

Time: 00:26

Date: 28.10.2015

So, you say, "I want to learn how to eat pussy?"
Well, come here and let me teach you how to boogie.
Lay her body down and open her legs wide,
Let's explore her pleasure with nothing to hide.

~

First, start by caressing her inner thighs,
Ignite the fire within as desire intensifies.
Gently tease her clit, don't be afraid,
Show her pleasure that cannot be swayed.

~

Now, slide your fingers inside her tight space,
Make sure it's wet and ready for a passionate chase.
Be gentle and attentive as you explore,
Don't rush the journey, let pleasure soar.

~

Next, pay attention to her sensitive breasts,
Use your tongue to bring forth intense zest.
Make that pussy sign with your skilled tongue,
Show her ecstasy till she realises that this is not for fun.

~

Remember, it's about pleasure and connection too,
Respect boundaries and always communicate what's true.
With desire and consent guiding the way,
You'll learn how to eat pussy like a pro one day.

~

As you caress her breasts with tender care,
Lock eyes with her, a passionate stare.
Feel the warmth of her pussy, inviting and sweet,
It's time to explore, to taste and greet.

~

Gently, your tongue glides down her skin,
Savouring every moment, a sensual sin.
She whispers in pleasure, lost in the bliss,
As you pleasure her pussy, a divine abyss.

~

Explore her clit with skilful precision,
Unlocking desires, an erotic mission.
With each lick and flick, she quivers and moans,
Her pleasure intensifies, passion now sown.

~

Pressing your lips against her thighs so fine,
Size doesn't matter when it's ecstasy time.
Her legs wrap around you, cries fill the air,
In this moment of intimacy, nothing to spare.

~

You've completed task one with success,
Now your lips can't hide or suppress,
She'll crave your oral touch, no doubt,
As you explore what she's about.

~

Her desire will grow and intensify,
She'll become addicted, no need to pry,
Your skilful licking will drive her wild,
And make her fantasies come alive.

Basic Nutrition

Time: 23:21

Date: 22.10.2015

As I lay there slumbering with my eyes so tightly sealed,
He softly murmurs, "Darling, can I devour your every meal?"
"May I ravage that derriere with passion and zeal?"
My senses awaken, my body now revealed.

~

As my pussy starts to listen, and my body wakes up,
I realized that it was morning, and he's about to crack a nut.

~

I rolled over quite gently,
But, my body attitude said "WHAT?"
My body wasn't scared of him, or his big dinosaur stuff.

~

With a twinkle in my eye and a sly little smile,
I whispered softly, "Let's make this morning worthwhile."
His eyes widened, filled with desire and lust,
As he eagerly replied, "Oh baby, you know I must."

~

Our bodies intertwined in a passionate embrace,
Exploring each other's pleasure with grace.
In the morning light, our love came alive,
As we revelled in the ecstasy that would thrive.

~

I lie there, caressing his head, allowing him to feast,
Whispering, "Yes, that's right, baby, you are a beast."

My legs tremble in pleasure as intensity increased,
But never will I close them; this pleasure won't cease.

Dawn's Delight

Time: 20:38
Date: 15.10.2015

I want to feel your kisses in the morning,
Pat me down, stretch me out while I'm yawning.
I can hear your heart beating as you're snoring,
Taking off your clothes, my desire soaring.

~

Baby, you're the one who makes my body quake,
Exploring every inch of me, no mistake.
Your touch ignites a fire that I can't fake,
Leaving me breathless, my knees start to shake.

~

You know just how to please me, that's for sure,
With every touch and caress, you allure.
From oral delights to positions obscure,
You satisfy my cravings and make them pure.

~

So come on baby, let's indulge tonight,
In passionate moments that feel so right.
Together we'll explore new heights,
And make love until the morning light.

Next-Door Chronicles

Time: 06:35
Date: 17.10.2015

I want to make sure your neighbours know my name,
As you scream in pleasure, letting them see your flame.
Pulling your hair, gripping your behind,
No shame in our game, passion intertwined.
Your pussy burning up, desire set ablaze,
Our sex so intense, leaving no room for praise.

~

I've never experienced a girl quite like you,
Your pussy stays the same, always wet and true.
I ravage your ass, driving you insane,
Leaving you breathless, unable to contain.

~

If you thought you were the best, oh how you're wrong,
It's not a joke, babe, this pleasure is strong.
So let the echoes of your screams fill the night air,
Let the neighbours know my name without a care.
Don't mistake me for a boy;
I'm a man through and through,
And I'll show you things that'll make your fantasies come true.

~

So next time you want to run your mouth,
Get to know what you've claimed.
I've got a big dick, and I know how to please it,
My skills are untamed.
And trust me when I tell you.
Your pussy won't be the same.

Enigma

Time: 17:02

Date: 16.10.2015

I have sex with you a lot in my head,
Got me twisting, got me turning,
Got me wetting up my bed.
When I close my eyes, I see your face,
Feeling your hands all over me, at a steady pace.

~

In my fantasies, we explore new heights,
Exploding with pleasure like fireworks on summer nights.
I imagine your lips on mine, kissing so sweet,
And the way you make me moan with your tongue's gentle beat.

~

As my nipple gets harder, and my pussy gets red,
I can imagine you deep inside of me, tears is what I will shed.
In this passionate embrace, our bodies entwined,
Exploring new depths of pleasure, our desires aligned.

~

My body trembles with anticipation and desire,
Longing for the moment when our passions ignite like fire.
Every touch, every stroke sends shivers down my spine,
As we lose ourselves in the rhythm and intertwine.

~

The thought of your mouth exploring every inch of my skin,
Leaves me breathless and craving to feel you deep within.
And when I think of how you devour me in every way,
I can't help but yearn for the ecstasy that comes into play.

~

So let's dance together in this erotic embrace,
Leaving behind the world as we find our sacred space.

In this sensual symphony where our bodies become one,
We'll create a masterpiece that will never be undone.

Rough Waters

Time: 17:20

Date: 16.10.2015

Choke me, Spank me,
Pull the weave from my hair.
Put it in deep boy, be unfair.
Fuck me so good that my body will disappear,
Losing all my breath, I am gasping for air.

~

As you lay there on the bed,
Your body shaven, so bare,
Caress my breasts with tender care,
Let's create a passionate affair.

~

Whisper dirty words in my ear, ignite the flames of desire,
Exploring pleasures we both aspire,
Our connection burning like fire.

~

Slap my ass and fuck me good, oh baby, make me scream,
Indulge in fantasies that we both deem,
Fulfilling each other's dream.

~

Taste the sweetness between my thighs,
As I moan with delight,
An oral symphony played all night, taking us to new heights.

~

Embrace the essence of our lust,
Entwined in a passionate dance,

With every touch and every glance,
We'll lose ourselves in a trance.

~

Explore uncharted territories,
Push boundaries beyond measure,
In this intimate treasure trove of pleasure and leisure.

~

Caress my curves with your tongue,
Let me feel your desire,
As we set our inhibitions on fire,
Letting passion take us higher.

~

Indulge in this ass, a feast for our senses,
Unlocking hidden pleasures behind closed fences.

~

Together we'll create an erotic masterpiece,
That leaves us breathless,
A symphony of love and lust,
Blended seamlessly in togetherness.
So let's embrace our desires without restraint or shame,
And ignite a flame that forever burns bright in our name.

Sex Symbol

Time: 05:25

Date: 17.10.2015

I want to be your sex symbol, the one who drives you wild,
Lay you down gently, as if I'm a poet with words so mild.
I'll lick you up and down, exploring every inch of your skin,
Never keeping it simple, let our passion begin.

~

Fuck me until I am old and gray,
until time has taken its toll,
Our love will only grow stronger,
a fire that never grows cold.
Caress my wrinkled skin with your tender touch,
For our connection transcends age, it means so much.

~

Oh, how I adore when you stand tall and proud,
Your dimples highlighting the smile that makes me feel endowed.
Like dogs in heat, let's mingle and intertwine,
Unleashing desires that are simply divine.

~

Make my eyes roll back with pleasure untamed,
Tremble my entire being, leave me forever changed.
On my nipples you'll feast, with a nimble touch,
Bringing ecstasy to life, we'll enjoy it so much.

~

Whisper dirty words in my ear,
make them twinkle like stars above,

As we explore the depths of passion and embrace this love.
After tonight, know that you're no longer alone,
Together we'll create a symphony that is all our own.

~

Where's the pen?
Where's the paper?
Where's the fucking pencil?
So weak in the knees,
But here's my number; take it as essential.
Baby, let's write a story of pleasure and delight,
In this journey of intimacy, let us both ignite.

Forbidden Temptations

Time: 01:18
Date: 15.10.2015

I want to fuck you like we're in a movie,
Sit back and just rewind while you do me.
I saw you walking down the road,
You were a cutie,
Now that we're together, let's climb into my Jacuzzi.

~

Baby, I want you all to myself, no groupie,
Sex so great, it got us feeling all woozy,
But let's explore beyond the usual play,
Embrace new pleasures, in our own special way.

~

I'll eat your pussy like a delicacy,
With each lick, bringing you to ecstasy.
And when it's time for some rear delight,
I'll lick your ass with all my might.

~

Let me caress your breasts with tender care,
As I tease and please them, making you gasp for air.
Together we'll indulge in passionate desire,
Setting each other's bodies on fire.

~

So let's dive deep into this erotic bliss,
Exploring fantasies that we simply can't resist.
In this intimate dance, we'll find pure satisfaction.
Sex so good the movie will never be a distraction.

Oral Delight

Time: 19:58
Date: 11/03/24

Drink up baby girl, you'll be rising with the sun,
No time for games, we're done having fun.
We've reached a stage where flirting's passé,
But that doesn't mean we can't find new ways to play.

~

So let's explore the realms of oral delight,
Kissing and touching, igniting the night.
Forget about age and any insecurity,
In this moment, we're free to express our sensuality.

~

Together we'll discover pleasure anew,
With every touch, every kiss, every taboo.
No need to worry about what comes next,
Let's lose ourselves in passion and forget the rest.

~

So come closer my love, let's make memories tonight,
Exploring desires that feel oh so right.
In this intimate dance, our bodies entwined,
We'll find ecstasy together, leaving inhibitions behind.

Rough, Raw & Ready

Time: 05:44

Date: 17.10.2015

I'm lying here, rough, raw & ready,
Awaiting your arrival, oh so steady.
Step through the door and say "Chevy,"
For I crave your touch, don't keep me waiting, baby.

~

Your kisses ignite a fire deep within,
Undressing you slowly, let the passion begin.
With each moan and gasp, our desires intertwine,
In this heated moment, our bodies align.

~

Exploring each other's pleasure zones with delight,
Oral sensations that take us to new heights.
No need to hide behind sheets or be discreet,
Let's indulge in the pleasures we both seek.

~

As I taste your sweetness and you lick my skin,
We'll lose ourselves in this erotic rhythm.
Breathless and sweaty, our bodies entwined,
In this raw connection, pure pleasure we find.

~

So come through the door and let's fulfil our desires,
Together we'll create a symphony of passionate fires.
No need to eat spaghetti on the plate,
Just eat me instead, indulging in love's sweetest state.

Libido Boost

Time: 03:47
Date: 16.10.2015

I have a high sex d**rive,**
I've created my own imagination,
It's like, my body and my soul,
Has been locked up in **incarceration**.

~

You are feeling on my breast,
Making your very own **creation**,
I love it when you lay me down, and tell me to "fuck the **conversation**".

~

Your sex has me feeling so good,
It is like an **hallucination**,
My body is so weak,
But, I can't stop the **temptation**.

Baby if you leave me now, I will die in **devastation**,
I haven't ate in days, so I guess it's **starvation**.

~

When you're rubbing on my clit, there is no **explanation**,
Feeling on my spot, that could be your **destination**.

~

I will let the whole world know,
I will tell the **fucking nation,**
Let them all know what you're about,
Let them start their **fascination**.

~

You are all mine, God has made you my very own **creation**,
And every single day, I will enjoy you in **celebration**.

Neutral Territory

Time: 02:24

Date: 16.10.2015

Let me tell you this, Baby the feeling is neutral.
Having you around for a while, was useful.
You can never break my heart,
Because I am strong, I am brutal,
I know you dislike me, but the feeling is mutual.

~

But let's not dwell on negativity and hostility,
Instead, let's explore the realm of sensuality.
I'll take you to heights you've never known before,
With every touch and kiss leaving you craving for more.

~

I'll tease and please with my oral skills so divine,
Making your body quiver and your senses intertwine.
And when it comes to pussy eating, I'm a master,
Bringing waves of pleasure faster and faster.

~

But don't think it stops there, my love knows no bounds,
I'll indulge in ass licking that will make you astound.
With each stroke and lick of my tongue so sweet,
I'll have you begging for release, completely at my feet.

~

My love is like a fire, strong and commanding,
I'll pleasure you like no one else, understanding.
Your desires, your needs, I'll satisfy them all,

Leaving you breathless, begging for more, enthralled.

~

Having you gathering evidence, like it was crucial,
Exploring every inch of you, leaving no detail residual.
Discovering new pleasures, hidden depths within,
Our intimate moments, a passionate dance we begin.

~

You'll think "damn, she's wild", as I push the limits,
Unleashing fantasies that will leave you in fits.
Yes, baby boy, I'll have you under my spell,
Craving my touch, addicted to the way I excel.

~

And when it's time for breast and dick to meet,
The passion we ignite will be oh so sweet.
So baby, let go of inhibitions and come explore,
The depths of pleasure we can both adore.

The Art of Learning

Time: 04:11

Date: 17.10.2015

Eat her like a queen, but make love to her soul,
Caress every inch of her, making her whole.
Explore the depths of passion, a journey untold.
~

Fuck her like a slut, unleash primal desire,
Leave no fantasy unfulfilled, set her heart on fire.
Tease and please, taking her higher and higher.
Make that dick go all the way up in her gut,
Ignite the flames of pleasure, intense and hot.
A dance of ecstasy, connecting body and thought.
~

Lay her on the table, a canvas for your touch,
Create art with your hands, expressing so much.
Whisper sweet nothings as you make her blush.
~

Now bend her over backwards, embrace the wild,
Thrill in the wickedness, let inhibitions be defiled.
In this moment of passion, you both are beguiled.
~

There's no if, no maybes, just pure connection,
A symphony of bodies in perfect reflection.
An intimate dance, filled with affection.
~

It's just you and her body, an erotic symphony,
No remorse or regrets as you explore so freely.
Lost in each other's arms, time stands still completely.
~

And when you're finished with her body's desire,
Unlock the door to her mind and set it on fire.
Discover the depths of intellect that inspire.

~
It's just you and her mind now in this sacred space,
Engage in conversation that leaves no trace.
Connecting on a level that words can't replace.
~

So go ahead and order some pizza hut,
Replenish your energy after this passionate rut.
Savouring the moments shared without any cut.

Nourish & Thrive

Time: 16:43

Date: 16.10.2015

I want you to turn her around, and eat that pussy.
There is no need to be rough,
But, you can be a little pushy.

~

Got her turned over, ass up in the air,
Ready for you to devour with care.
Softly kissing her thighs,
Making her moan with pleasure as time flies.

~

She's been waiting for this moment all day,
Shaved and clean, ready to play.
Tasting her sweetness with every lick,
Driving her wild with each flick.

~

You explore every inch of her delicate skin,
Teasing and pleasing with a devilish grin.
As your tongue dances on her sensitive mound,
She writhes beneath you without a sound.

~

Your oral skills bring her to the edge of bliss,
Her body quivering from the pleasure you've missed.
Orgasmic waves crash through her core,
Leaving her craving for more and more.

~

So go ahead and indulge in this naughty delight,
Embrace your desires and make her night.
Just remember to always respect and please,
And give her pleasure that will bring her to her knees.

Big Fat Extravaganza

Time: 03:58
Date: 17.10.2015

I want to be bouncing on your thick hard cock,
As you're thrusting deep inside, it's like a sweet shock.
I can feel the pleasure building up, making me moan,
Your touch on my clit sends shivers to the bone.

~

The pleasure builds and builds, reaching its peak,
I can feel my orgasm coming, so sweet and unique.
I'm losing control, my senses going wild,
As I surrender to pleasure, I feel like a child.

~

You're all I ever wanted, my ultimate desire,
Our passion ignites like a burning fire.
But this moment feels too good to be true,
Like a dream come alive, just me and you.

~

I'm a lady in the streets, but with you I'm wild,
Unleashing all our fantasies like an untamed child.
Together we explore the depths of ecstasy's abyss,
Indulging in desires that we both cannot resist.
So let's surrender to our passions tonight,
And create a memory that feels oh so right.

~

Oh baby, come closer and let's make this night divine,
Our bodies entwined as we reach cloud nine.

Excitement

Time: 02:00

Date: 14.10.2015

Sometimes, the body just craves a touch of thrill,
A spark to ignite its fire, a moment to fulfil.
It yearns to bloom and flourish like a rose,
To feel alive and vibrant, from head to toes.

~

It longs for exploration and new sensations,
To be caressed with love, in different locations.
With gentle strokes and whispers so divine,
It seeks pleasure that's intoxicating like fine wine.

~

A skilled lover who knows how to please,
With oral delights that bring it to its knees.
From pussy eating that leaves it weak and trembling,
To ass licking that sets its senses assembling.

~

The breasts crave attention, soft kisses and bites,
While the dick yearns for release, explosive nights.
In this dance of passion, the body finds release,
A symphony of desire where pleasure never cease.

Art of Romancing

Time: 01:41
Date: 14.10.2015

Love is not just about the romantic gestures,
It's about finding a partner who truly invests,
In your dreams and goals, supporting your every move,
And dancing through life together, in the groove.

~

Yes, finances can be a concern in any relationship,
But love is not solely defined by monetary worship.
It's about understanding, trust, and emotional connection,
Advancing together, overcoming any financial tension.

~

You can make her feel special without spending a dime,
By simply unmasking your true self, it's sublime.
Light some candles to create an intimate ambiance,
Buy her favourite flowers, show your love in abundance.

But beyond the material things, there lies a deeper need,
To touch her with passion, fulfilling her desire indeed.
As she bathes under your loving gaze and tender touch,
Her knees grow weak with pleasure, she wants you so much.

~

Let the music play loud, creating a sensual vibe,
As you explore each other's bodies with a passionate drive.
For in these moments of intimacy and connection so pure,
She realizes that this is all she ever longed for, for sure.

~

So remember, love is not just about romance or lust,
It's about finding that soulmate with whom you're entrust.
Together you dance through life's ups and downs,
Creating a love story that knows no bounds.

Jackpot Dick

Time: 03:41
Date: 17.10.2015

~~~

Fuck my mind, and my body will follow,
Left, right, front, back; fuck waking up tomorrow.
I see your head in between my legs,
Do you savour every taste or just beg?
Let's explore the depths of pleasure's flow,
With each touch and stroke, our desires grow.

~

Do you spit, or do you swallow?
I know you've got a girl, but tonight I'm your Apollo.
Let's indulge in a passionate affair, no need to be coy,
I'll give you pleasure that will make your heart jump with joy.

~

From oral delights to deep, satisfying penetration,
I'll explore every inch of you,
fulfilling each naughty temptation.
Together we'll reach heights of ecstasy,
leaving us both in a state of bliss,
So let's forget about the world and embark on this carnal abyss.

~

I feel your presence, electrifying and intense,
As we delve into a world of sensual suspense.
No inhibitions, no boundaries to restrict,

Just pure pleasure and passion that intermix.
Exploring new realms with every thrust,
Our bodies entwined in a fiery lust.

~

In this moment of unbridled bliss,
I crave your touch, your warmth, your kiss.
We dance together in a rhythm so divine,
Each movement igniting a primal shine.
Lost in the ecstasy of our carnal play,
Bodies yearning for more with every sway.

~

So let us embrace this wild desire,
Fuelling the flames that burn higher and higher.
No shame or judgment can hold us back,
For it's in these moments we find what we lack.
In this realm where pleasure reigns supreme,
We create a world where fantasy becomes our theme.

Bruised & Amused

Time: 00:54

Date: 17.10.2015

Sex so rough, you've got me covered in bruises,
Bite me, fuck me, drink my juices.
Eat that pussy up, boy, no excuses,
I love it when you act like you're abusive.

~

In this bedroom war, we both surrender,
Exploring desires with passion so tender.
Embracing the pleasure and pain we render,
Leaving us yearning for more each time we enter.

~

No pain, no gain, as the saying goes,
We push our limits and expose,
The depths of our desires that nobody knows,
In this dance of pleasure where ecstasy flows.

~

Play with my clit, tease it to perfection,
Lick it up as you choose with affection.
Our bodies entwined in a passionate connection,
Lost in the moment, powering our obsession.

~

We are warriors of lust, never to lose,
The pain we endure only further amuse.
With every touch and every bruise,
We indulge in pleasures that nothing defuse.

Less is More

Time: 01:12

Date: 17.10.2015

When she enters through the door,
I want you to start off by stripping.
Then lay her body down,
With your tongue, you'll be exploring.

~

If she's trying to move her body,
And act like she's fucking tripping,
Then take control and guide her, make sure she's not slipping.

~

Don't let her doubt your intentions,
Show her you're committed,
In the next position, pleasure her with oral and get her uplifted.

~

As you explore deeper inside of her,
Embrace the pleasure you're bringing,
Her moans and gasps tell you there's something amazing she's experiencing.

~

Her mind is in a frenzy, her body trembling and shaking,
Keep up the rhythm, keep going, there's no time for faking.

~

That's it, keep going strong, feel the intensity building,
Soon you'll both reach climax, passion and desire fulfilling.

~

Explore every inch and crevice,
With gentle strokes and caresses.
Tease her senses, make her quiver,
As you taste her pleasure, deliver.

~

Deliver pleasure with every lick,
Igniting fires that begin to flick.
Her moans crescendo, filling the air,
As you navigate her body with care.

~

Carefully now, guide her to the bed,
Where passion and desire are fed.
Positioned perfectly, side by side,
In this moment, there's nowhere to hide.

~

Hidden desires unravel and unfold,
As together you both lose control.
The rhythm intensifies as bodies collide,
In a symphony of pleasure that cannot hide.

~

With each thrust, the connection deepens,
As ecstasy within her body awakens.
Moans and whispers fill the room,
As you both reach climax in a sonic boom.

Art That Strips

Time: 19:47
Date: 11/03/24

Lights dimmed low, an intimate scene,
We're lost in passion, a perfect routine.
With every move, our bodies entwined,
Exploring pleasure, our desires aligned.

~

I caress your skin, like a poet's touch,
Each stroke and kiss, I love so much.
In the darkness, our connection grows,
A symphony of moans, passion flows.

~

Your hardness throbbing against my luscious lips,
I take you in eagerly, like an art that strips.
Our rhythm harmonizes, a sensual dance,
As we find ecstasy in each passionate glance.

~

Time flies by as we explore new heights,
The fruits of pleasure blooming through the nights.
No matter the season, our love remains strong,
In your arms, I know where I belong.

~

So fuck me with ardour, leave me breathless and wild,
Our love-making transcends any definition or style.
In this intimate space where boundaries cease,
We create poetry with every touch and release.

Sex Life Unfiltered

Time: 02:00
Date: 17.10.2015

Sex life so great, Got us looking all flawless.
Lay me down, Spread me out, fuck me,
You're hardest.

~

Exploring new positions, we've never tried,
Your expertise takes us on a wild ride.
With your impressive member, so grand,
It feels like the largest in the land.

~

In complete darkness, our bodies entwined,
Passionate moans fill the air, no light to find.
I pleasure you skillfully, like an artist at play,
Rapping on your dick, in my own unique way.

~

As the seasons change, our love remains strong,
From winter's embrace to spring's sweet song.
No matter what you do, my love won't diminish,
You promised to fuck my brains out, and I believe every wish.

~

But don't worry, baby, your actions are kind,
Leaving my heart intact and my soul intertwined.
Feeling your hardness against me again and again,
It's a testament to our sexual chemistry; it will never wane.

Sex Past Thirty

Time: 06:00
Date: 17.10.2015

Fuck hard and talk dirty,
We are not old, Just past thirty.
Got my dick in your mouth,
And I know you're thirsty.
But let's take a moment,
To enjoy this pleasure bursty.

~

You're an expert at giving head,
Your skills, oh so worthy.
Don't worry about the clock,
Let's make this night lengthy.

~

We may be past the age,
To be all flirty flirty.
But we've found a new passion,
In exploring each other's dirty.

~

So let's push our limits,
And take our desires on a journey.
No need to think about tomorrow,
Let's escape to a place like Turkey.

Sex Preparation

Time: 21:38

Date: 15.10.2015

I need some inspiration,
Baby your love is my preparation.
With you, I feel a sensation,
A connection beyond explanation.

~

Your touch ignites my imagination,
Sending waves of pleasure in every location.
Our bodies intertwined, a perfect formation,
Exploring desires with no hesitation.

~

Kissing your lips, a sweet temptation,
Lost in the moment, pure elation.
Our love-making, a beautiful creation,
Leaving us both in a state of adoration.

~

In your arms, I find salvation,
A sanctuary from the world's frustration.
Together we explore our deepest fascination,
A passionate journey of exploration.

~

Baby I own you, so fuck all the irritation,
Got me dreaming about your body, and its reputation.
Stuck to you like glue, we're inseparable,
No distance can tear us apart, undeniable.

~

I'll even plan ahead, make reservations,
To ensure our time together exceeds expectations.
You've got me feeling alive, no room for relaxation,
Creating a future with you, a passionate dedication.
~

So let's embrace this intimate relation,
And indulge in our shared fixation.
For with you, there's no limitation,
Just pure bliss and satisfaction.

Sex Obsession

Time: 09:16
Date: 16.10.2015

If I don't get your sex, I will start to lose sleep,
Start staying up thinking, how you're a cheat.
But let's not dwell on that, let's focus on the pleasure we reap,
Exploring new sensations, our desires running deep.

~

Together we create a symphony of moans and sighs,
As I taste your sweetness with every stroke and rise.
Oral pleasures exchanged, as we lose ourselves in the highs,
Fulfilling fantasies, igniting passion that never dies.

~

In this intimate dance, our bodies entwined,
We explore each other's pleasure with a hunger so kind.
Whispering naughty words that play with our mind,
Leaving no inch untouched, no desire left behind.

~

So let us indulge in this sensual affair,
Embracing the ecstasy that fills the air.
No need to hide or pretend to be fair,
For in each other's arms, we find solace and care.

~

So come closer my love, let us embark on this journey,
Where pleasure and intimacy are bound by no attorney.
Let's revel in the moments where passion is unwary,
And create memories that leave us forever merry.

~

Got me staring in your face,
While I am trying to take a peep,
When you press that horn, it goes, beep, beep, beep.

I don't want to just treat you, like you are a piece of meat,
But, when you break it down slowly, my body starts to sweep.

~

You are definitely not just some sex, that is cheap,
But a talent in the bedroom,
And I never want to fall asleep.

~

Your touch ignites a fire within me, intense and deep,
As we explore new realms of passion and embrace.
In the realm of pleasure, together we'll leap,
Creating electric moments that we'll forever keep.

Through the Cracks

Time: 00:43

Date: 17.10.2015

It seems as if things are about to get a bit freaky,
If you are under 18, then you should maybe watch a movie.

~

He's whispering naughty words in my ear, making me feel
cheesy, Oh, the pleasure he brings, it's making me dizzy.

~

I crave your touch every day, it's addictive and sneaky,
Sneaking into my mind, making me want you weekly.

~

Thrusting harder, don't hold back, don't be timid or needy,
Exploring each other's bodies, feeling oh so greedy.

~

Caressing my inner thighs, exploring me completely,
In this moment of passion, we're both feeling freely.

~

Beads of sweat rolling down our skin so steamy,
Your love is like a feast for my senses, fulfilling and meaty.

~

You're my addiction, the drug that makes me go crazy,
Wrapped in your arms, I feel like your sweet little lady.

~

So let's surrender to this passion and make it all hazy,
With every touch and kiss, our desires come alive like a genie.

~

Your light skinned body, so smooth, never greasy,
Your lips have turned me into an addicted, damn I am needy.
I know that you'll be my drug, my sweet fantasy,
With every touch, you awaken a fire inside of me.

~

In your embrace, passion flares up like a burning flame,
Our bodies entwined, our desires we can't tame.
You're the genie of pleasure, granting my every wish,
As we explore new heights of ecstasy with each passionate kiss.

~

The room grows hotter, sweat dripping off our skin,
Lost in the rhythm of love, we let our inhibitions thin.
You're my addiction, and I crave your touch,
Together we create a symphony of pleasure that's just too much.

Sex Date

Time: 16:00

Date: 16.10.2015

Can I take you out on a date?
Buy you a nice dinner plate?
Then take you home and lay you down,
And make you feel great.

~

I know, it's only half past eight,
And, I am running a little late,
But, baby girl, I promise, I will never make you wait.

~

I see that you're a curvy girl,
But your body is a mesmerizing swirl,
I can't help but imagine how we'll unfurl.

~

I know that I am being forward and bold,
But your allure is too strong to withhold,
You have a presence that can never be sold.

~

So let's explore this connection and see where it leads,
Embracing the passion that our desire feeds,
Together we'll create moments no one else needs.

~

Then after dinner we could maybe go ice-skate,
You could then maybe, just maybe,
Let me take on the role of your date,
We'll glide hand in hand, our hearts intertwined,
As we twirl and spin, leaving worries behind.

~

Afterwards, we can find a cozy spot,
Where I can whisper sweet words that hit the right spot,
And if you're willing, I'll explore every inch,
With tender kisses and a touch that makes you flinch.

~

So let's embark on this passionate escapade,
Where desires are fulfilled and inhibitions fade,
Together we'll create a symphony of pleasure,
Leaving memories that we'll forever treasure.

CRAVING

Time: 16:13

Date: 16.10.2015

Your sex drive has me completely hooked,
I'm over here in the kitchen, pretending to cook.
When your pants come off, I can't help but look,
My desire for you is like an open book.

~

I'm captivated by your every move,
Intoxicated by your sensual groove.
You ignite a fire that I can't ignore,
Leaving me wanting more and more.

~

Every touch, every kiss, sends shivers down my spine,
With you, darling, pleasure is always mine.
In your arms, I find pure ecstasy,
Exploring each other so passionately.

~

So let's indulge in this seductive game,
Where our desires burn like a wild flame.
Together we'll create our own fantasy,
A world where pleasure reigns eternally.

Sex Potion

Time: 05:06

Date: 17.10.2015

Your sex, it plays games with my mind,
Leaving me lost and blind,
I'm caught up in your spell,
The way you work that magic, oh so well.

~

But I can't help but wonder,
Is it love or just lust that I'm under?
Your pussy potions have me hooked,
In a state of desire, completely shook.

~

I don't want anyone else to hold you tight,
I'll fight for you with all my might,
Rest assured, my love is true,
But damn, girl, what's your secret brew?

~

We dive deep into passion's sea,
Bodies entwined, setting us free,
Moans and whispers fill the air,
As we explore each other without a care.

~

Is this love or just a sexual storm?
From heartbreak to devotion, I transform.
Caught between emotions and desires unspoken,
Lost in the whirlwind of your love, heartbroken.

~

But I can't deny this connection we share,
Falling deeper in love, beyond compare.
I might have to give you a promotion in my heart,
For the way you've torn my world apart.

~

I must find a way to control these feelings inside,
To navigate this passion and take your pussy on a ride.
But until then, I surrender to your seductive notion,
Lost in your sex and those pussy potions.

Melodies of Desire

Time: 02:37
Date: 15.10.2015

The love inside of me, wanted to come out for so long,
But, there were so many people out there, telling me
"This is wrong".

~

But I ignored their voices, their judgment and their hate,
Because my heart knew that with you, it was fate.
You came into my life like a ray of light,
Bringing joy and happiness, making everything feel right.
In your arms, I found solace and peace,
A love so strong, it cannot cease.

~

Every moment with you is like a sweet melody,
A symphony of passion and ecstasy.
I want to explore every inch of your body,
To taste the pleasure that awaits, so naughty.

~

So let's embrace this love we've found,
And let our desires run wild and unbound.
Together we'll create a world of our own,
Where our love will forever be known.

~

Together we'll create a love story that's pure and divine,
No more hiding or pretending, our hearts will intertwine.
So let's embrace this love that's burning deep within,
And show the world that our love knows no sin.

The Art of Exhibitionism

Time: 00:37

Date: 23.10.2015

I want you to fuck me in a public place,
Drag me through the alley,
Use up all the space.
Let's find a spot where we can be discreet,
Where our passion and desire can freely meet.
In the shadows, we'll ignite a forbidden flame,
Leaving behind any sense of shame.

~

With urgency and fervour, we'll make our move,
Like two wild souls caught in a sensual groove.
Exploring each other with an ardent embrace,
Lost in the thrill of our intimate chase.
As the night surrounds us, we'll surrender to lust,
In this public rendezvous, our desires we trust.

~

No judgments shall hold us back or impede,
For in this moment, it's just you and me.
Together we'll create a symphony of pleasure,
A secret melody only we can treasure.
And when it's done, we'll vanish without a trace,
Leaving behind no evidence or misplaced lace.

~

So let's indulge in this daring escapade,
Where inhibitions fade and passion is displayed.
In this public realm where desires intertwine,
We'll break free from societal confines.
For love knows no boundaries or walls to encase,

So let's fuck in a public place.

~

Now from the alley, to the barn, Right back to a PUBLIC PLACE! You're so strong, damn baby, have you ever lift weights?

~

Now let's venture out into the night,
Exploring our desires with all our might.
In this clandestine rendezvous we embrace,
Unleashing passion in a rhythmic chase.

~

Our bodies intertwine like a poetic rhyme,
As we surrender to pleasure, sublime.
Whispering secrets in each other's ear,
Oral indulgence that brings us near.

~

In this dance of lust and raw desire,
We ignite flames that burn higher and higher.
Uninhibited and free, we find solace here,
In this PUBLIC PLACE where inhibitions disappear.

The Pleasure Palace

Time: 00:45

Date: 23.10.2015

I want to be your naughty little SEX TOY!
Fuck me hard, bring me pleasure and joy.
Take me to new heights, make me scream and moan,
In your hands, I'm yours to own.

~

Fuck me with passion, with fire and desire,
Set my body ablaze, make me feel higher.
With each thrust and touch, you ignite my soul,
Leaving me breathless, completely under your control.

~

You're the master of pleasure, the conductor of bliss,
Every touch from you is a sensual kiss.
You push my boundaries, explore every part,
Leaving no inch untouched in this intimate art.

~

I crave your touch, your passionate embrace,
You bring satisfaction at an unrivalled pace.
Together we create a symphony of pleasure,
With every moment spent together a treasure.

~

So take me in your arms and let's explore,
The depths of our desires that we both adore.
I want to be your naughty little SEX TOY,
Let's indulge in ecstasy and never be coy.

Playing for Pleasure

Time: 01:34
Date: 23.10.2015

Handcuff me to the bed,
Then blindfold me,
It's now time to spread my legs,
There's no one to save me.

~

Spread lotion on my skin,
Let the seduction begin,
In this realm of pleasure and sin,
Our desires we won't rescind.

~

It's now time to taste and explore,
With every touch, I want more,
Savouring the ecstasy we adore,
Our passion reaching its core.

~

You're playing with my senses so sweet,
As our bodies intertwine and meet,
Euphoria rising, a symphony of heat,
Together, our desires complete.

~

Now you've turned me around,
And you gave my ass a slap,
Oh fuck, I'm getting horny,
But all I can see is black.

~

Your touch is driving me wild,
In and out, your hands never lack,
My body bouncing with pleasure,
Yes, that's it, Jack.

~

As you tease my sensitive spots,
I struggle to hold back,
Tongue swirling in circles,
Damn it, an asthma attack.
Please remove this blindfold,
I can't handle this, Jack,
Now you're devouring my clit,
Yes, indulge in that snack.

~

I know we won't remember coming morning,
Our escapade will fade into the black,
But I'll always recall how you had me screaming out loud,
Oh fuck, eat my crack.

From Foreplay to Finale

Time: 00:59
Date: 23.10.2015

First step,
Fuck her until she apologizes for shit she ain't even done,
With every thrust, show her who's the one.

~

Face down, ass up, make her scream in pleasure,
Let her be your dirty little treasure.

~

Her moans fill the room as you explore,
The taste of ecstasy you both adore.

~

But don't let her go, keep her close to your side,
In this passionate dance, let love be your guide.

~

Take your time, savour each moment and touch,
For in this intimate connection, there is so much.

~

Now she's begging for more, saying you've gone too far,
But you know deep inside you're about to reach a new star.

~

Keep going strong, my friend, until the finish line is won,
Because rough sex is better when it's with the one.

~

ROUGH SEX is better when you know she is the one,
Because even though you love her,
You know that sex is not for fun.

~

She is coming, Pussy twitching,
She's surprise, actually stunned.
She can't take it, It's time to break it,
She's now thinking about becoming a faithful nun.

~

But deep down inside, she craves the thrill,
The way he dominates, the power he instils.
Her body yearns for his rough touch,
A connection so intense, it's almost too much.

~

In these moments of passion and desire,
Their love ignites like a burning fire.
They explore their limits, pushing boundaries anew,
Knowing that in each other's arms, they found something true.

Big Dirty Dick's Diary

Time: 22:28
Date: 22.10.2015

I'm a hopeless romantic, with a big dirty dick,
But there's more to me than just this stick.
I'll sweep you off your feet, make your heart race,
And take you to places where passion finds its grace.

~

Let's delve into a world of intimate desire,
Where fantasies ignite and sparks catch fire.
Undress our inhibitions and let them fall away,
As we explore each other in the most sensual way.

~

I'll hold you close against the wall so tight,
Whispering sweet words as we lose ourselves in the night.
Together, we'll create a symphony of pleasure,
As our bodies entwine, finding ultimate treasure.

~

So don't be fooled by my big dirty dick,
For behind it lies a lover who knows how to click.
Open wide and let me into your soul,
As we embark on a journey that will make us both whole.

Sex Power

Time: 23:34
Date: 25.10.2015

As you step into the bedroom,
I want you to fuck me in the shower.
Let the steam rise, bodies entwined,
Passion flowing, desires aligned.
Water cascading, a sensual dance,
Our moans harmonizing in this chance.
A wet embrace, pleasure's symphony,
Our love story written in liquid poetry.

~

Use up all your strength baby,
Show me all your power.
Don't be kissing on my ass,
Like I'm a delicate little flower,
It's nearly half past six,
And I have to get up in an hour.

~

But let's not waste time with trivialities,
Let's explore the depths of our desires,
No need for sweet talk or pleasantries,
Unleash the passion that fuels our fires.

~

From the bed to the chair, we'll make our way,
Exploring every surface, no corner left untouched,
With each moment, our connection will sway,
As we surrender to pleasure, completely unclutched.

~

You're licking on my clit,
As I'm feeling all your manpower.
This has to be heaven,
Or maybe, it's happy hour.

~

Your tongue moves with a rhythmic grace,
Sending waves of pleasure through my space.
In this moment, we create our own symphony,
A passionate dance of ecstasy.

~

The taste of you lingers on my lips,
As our bodies entwine in a sensual eclipse.
Every touch ignites a fiery desire,
Fueling the flames of our passionate fire.

~

Lost in the depths of pure bliss,
Our connection transcends the physical, amiss.
Time stands still as we explore and play,
In this sacred space, where pleasure holds sway.

Forbidden Desires

Time: 23:57
Date: 25.10.2015

I understand that you may still be involved with your wife,
But baby, let's have our own secret sex life.
I can imagine the passion between us, so intense and rare,
With every touch and kiss, we'll ignite a fiery affair.
Bend me over on the couch, as your pulling on my hair,
From the bed, To the kitchen, no fuck it, let's go over there.

~

As you step inside my realm, behold, my pussy is primed.
Never faltering, it requires no mending, no need to be timed.
Oh, let us envision ourselves amidst a cascading stream,
A bathroom seat our throne, fulfilling every whim and dream.
I'll bounce upon your dick, as you whisper words of care,
Exploring positions aplenty, a symphony of pleasure in the air.

~

Your skilled tongue dances on my earlobe,
Igniting flames within,
And as we intertwine beneath the shower's gentle din.
Our bodies drenched in liquid bliss,
Water trickling through our hair,
The ecstasy we share is beyond compare.

~

Your prowess with your member is an art form to embrace,
Leaving your wife yearning for a taste of such grace.
My nipples tingle under your touch,
Leaving me breathless and weak,
Water caressing our skin as passion reaches its peak.

~

I am watching you, pondering why life seems so unjust,
Your wife better keep an eye on me, for in her I'll entrust.
She must be cautious and fully aware,
Of the desires that simmer beneath my stare.

~

In this game of lust and temptation,
I offer a feast, a sweet sensation.
For I possess the skill of oral delight,
To pleasure your senses throughout the night.

Pussy Riot

Time: 23:32

Date: 25.10.2015

I want you to ravage my pussy so intense,
Ignite a passion that's too immense.
Fuck it up, make me scream your name,
Leave me breathless, drenched in pleasure's flame.

~

With each thrust and every squeeze,
Take me to heights I've never reached, please.
Don't hold back, let our desires ignite,
As we dance in the darkness, bodies entwined tight.

~

My ass in the air, ready for your touch,
A balance of power, an intoxicating rush.
Feed my hunger, fulfil my appetite,
For this forbidden pleasure we both invite.

~

Beat it up, leave no room for rest,
Consume me whole, I'm yours to possess.
Like David against Goliath's might,
Our love knows no boundaries, day or night.

~

My pussy roars with a primal sound,
As you explore every inch that's found.
Treat me like a queen, show me your devotion,
For in your arms is where I find true emotion.

~
This poetry we create is like a sonnet by Wyatt,
A masterpiece of pleasure that feels so right.
Your dick has the power to ignite my fire,
And keep me moaning with unquenchable desire.

Mind Games

Time: 00:43
Date: 26.10.2015

So, you're coming all up in here,
Shouting your head off.
But, baby, I ain't lying, you look like a boss.

~

I could devour every inch of you,
Savouring every taste,
With every lick and nibble, time would be erased.

~

Mmm, the way you fume and glare,
It sets my soul ablaze,
In the heat of our passion, we'll explore uncharted ways.

~

Right now, I swear I'd tie you up, unleash your wildest desires, Indulging in pleasure that ignites like raging fires.

~

You're a vision of fierce beauty when you're mad,
A force to reckon with, never making me sad.

~

Oh darling, the fantasies that dance inside my mind,
We'd traverse forbidden paths where ecstasy we'll find.

~

You're like a model when you're angry,
Looking a bit like Kate Moss,
Oh, the things that I would do to you,
I would have to double cross.
You're standing there talking, with your shiny lip gloss,
But my thoughts are wandering to places untamed,
Imagining the taste of your skin, so soft and boss,
In my mind, a wild desire has been inflamed.

~

I envision myself exploring every inch of you,
With passion and intensity, no detail missed,
The way you move, the way you moan, it's true,
My imagination runs wild with a fervent twist.

~

Oh, how I long to bring you pleasure supreme,
To taste your sweetness like a forbidden treat,
In this fantasy world, our bodies would gleam,
As I indulge in the art of pussy eating with heat.

Sex Reward

Time: 00:57
Date: 26.10.2015

I don't seek tender affection,
I crave raw passion, no objection.
Handle me like you're intoxicated,
No inhibitions, no defenses barricaded.

~

Tonight, I'll take you on a wild ride,
But remember, I'll sleep by your side.
Bind your hands, leave marks on your skin,
Indulge in pleasure that's deemed a sin.

~

You'll moan my name, cry out in bliss,
As if it's the sweetest melody you can't dismiss.
My dick is unmatched, it won't be denied,
Leaving you intoxicated long after the ride.

~

Even when it's done, don't brush it aside,
Our connection lingers, impossible to hide.
Don't think you can manipulate or deceive,
I lay my cards down, make you believe.
And in the end, fulfil my desire,
Let me taste your passion, set me on fire.

Awakened

Time: 01:16

Date: 26.10.2015

I see your seductive gaze fixed on me,
like a game of desire you're keeping score,
As we enter round two, our passion intensifies, craving for more.

~

Once upon a time,
Your innocence adorned your sacred space,
Now you've blossomed into a sensual being,
Embracing pleasure with grace.

~

Our moans echo through the walls,
Arousing curiosity next door,
But the ecstasy we create is worth every knock on my door.

~

You, my enchanting muse, speak of exploring uncharted lands, With each rhythmic motion, we soar beyond earthly demands.

~

1, 2, 3... and soon we'll reach an ecstasy so divine, Our bodies entwined in blissful harmony, reaching cloud nine.

~

Now you're bouncing on my dick,
Oh girl, I really can't ignore,
How the fuck will I ever walk to the grocery store?
Dick sucking, pussy gripping,
You are going hardcore.

~

But it shocked me to the bones,
When you told me "there was more".
In that moment of pure bliss,
I knew I had opened a new door.
Exploring depths of pleasure untold,
Our connection grew stronger than before.

Carnal Connections

Time: 01:40

Date: 26.10.2015

God only knows that our sex life was interconnected,
In the bedroom,
You fulfilled all my desires,
I elected.
You were everything I craved,
Every fantasy, you perfected.

~

In your embrace, I found solace,
In your passion, I felt protected.
Our connection was electric,
Every touch left me breathless and affected.

~

With you, pleasure was guaranteed,
Never had to worry about being neglected.
Your oral skills were unmatched,
Leaving me satisfied and resurrected.

~

But as we went our separate ways,
I had to reflect and introspect.
It wasn't love that bound us together,
Just a physical bond we both respected.

~

I will remember your touch,
But never get affective, I knew that you loved me,
But your love, I rejected.
See, I knew you were the one,
You were the best I've ever selected,
Got me dreaming about your touch,
It was amazing, PERFECTED!

~

I'm sorry that we didn't work out,
But our love never connected,
I hated your personality,
But your sex, I respected.

~

You know it's YOU!
That I am talking about,
Yes, this message is directed.

~

I am sorry I broke your heart,
But, you could have never been collective.

Sensual Canvas

Time: 23:57

Date: 27.10.2015

Why don't you let me,
Lay your body down, and give it a few loving strokes?
Then we can dip into the water,
As our passion ignites and evokes.

~

Darling, I assure you, this is no game,
I'm not here to play with your heart or provoke.

~

I'm reaching out to find out,
If you're alone, in the comfort of your own abode.

~

And if the coast is clear, my love,
Let's share intimate moments and explode.

~

We'll explore the depths of pleasure,
Using our bodies as a means to decode.

~

Making love all through the night,
Whispering prayers as our connection erodes,
Hoping your guardians won't stumble upon us,
Indulging in each other's touch, unopposed.

Possessed by You

Time: 01:54
Date: 26.10.2015

If I'm pleasuring your desires,
I won't let anyone else share.
My focus is solely on you,
No distractions, no one to interfere.

~

I truly couldn't care less,
About what others may say or declare.
With every touch and kiss,
I'll make you swear, beyond compare.

~

If another tries to claim what's mine,
I'll protect your pleasure, Claire.
For your satisfaction is my devotion,
A connection we both willingly declare.

~

In my eyes, it's a sacred bond,
A testament of love and care.
So rest assured, my dear,
Your pleasure is my only affair.

~

No need for worry or doubt,
Your satisfaction I will ensnare.

Nothing compares to this intimacy,
A amazing experience we both share.

~

There is nothing else like it,
How can you compare?
Got a motherfucker gasping for breath,
I am trying to catch air.

Girl, I love it so much, I could never find a spare.
I don't care if there is better, I don't care if more is near.
So, let's sit down and talk,
Let's lay it out right here.
That's my pussy,
My nookie, It has now been declared.

Horny Horizons

Time: 21:00

Date: 27.10.2015

Let's call this one, the raging bull,
Grab her by the hair, and see how hard you can pull.
Put that tongue to work, exploring every fold,
Taste her sweetness, make her heart race and her body unfold.

~

Slide that cock in deep, make her moan and groan,
As she clings to the sheets, her pleasure is shown.

~

Explore every inch of her silky skin,
Tease her senses, let the ecstasy begin.
Whisper sweet nothings in her ear,
As you ignite a passion that's crystal clear.

~

Now slide your fingers inside,
Feel her wetness embrace,
Whisper dirty words in her ear,
Watch desire light up her face.
Kiss and lick her thighs, make her tremble and quake,
Her pleasure is your mission,
No limits or boundaries to break.

~

She arches her back as you devour her with grace,
The taste of her essence lingers on your tongue as you trace.
With each flick and swirl, she's lost in a world of bliss,
Pleasure pulsating through her veins with every gentle kiss.

~

No need for remorse or regrets in this intimate dance,
Just two souls intertwining in a passionate romance.
So go ahead and savour the Flavors of ecstasy,
In this moment of intimacy, let your desires run free.

Fatal Lust

Time: 20:38
Date: 27.10.2015

─────── ❧❧ ───────

I want you to leave my pussy in agony,
Leave it on its death bed,
What a tragedy.
Fuck me so hard, make my body quake,
Leave me breathless, in a state of ache.

~

I'll be begging for more, craving your touch,
Lost in the pleasure that you provide so much.
Every stroke and thrust, a symphony of delight,
Taking me to heights I've never reached in the night.

~

I'll be writhing beneath you, lost in ecstasy's embrace,
Moaning your name as you set my body ablaze.
You know just how to please me, how to make me moan,
Leaving my pussy satisfied and fully blown.

~

So let the world know of our passionate affair,
No need for secrecy or hiding what we share.
Your dick is like a masterpiece, a work of art,
And I'm addicted to every inch and every part.

~

Only you understand my deepest desires,

You fulfil them all with your passion that never tires.
Together we explore the realms of pleasure untold,
Leaving no fantasy unexplored or desire unsold.

~

I love you so much, You look after me financially.
And even though I'm in pain, I just love your generosity.

~

IF! I rise from this sickbed, my desires will be set free,
No more holding back, it's time for intensity,
I crave the passion, the heat, and the sensuality.

~

If I don't taste your oral pleasure,
I'll express my longing with fervour,
For when our bodies intertwine,
It's a symphony of pleasure that I savour.

~

In the depths of our connection, we find serenity,
Exploring each other's desires with pure transparency,
You fulfil my cravings, leaving no room for complacency.

The Sex Clutch Chronicles

Time: 20:49

Date: 27.10.2015

I'm a freak in the sheets,
And only you know how to tear that ass up.
But there's so much more to our sexual repertoire,
Let's explore and fill my cup.

~

In your eyes, I see desire burning like a flame,
Whispering sweet nothings, calling out each other's name.
But beyond the surface, deep down in my soul,
I crave your oral skills, baby, make me lose control.

~

Come closer, let me show you what I need,
Open up my legs and satisfy this insatiable greed.
I don't want diamonds or fancy things, Just your tongue
between my thighs, making my pleasure sing.

~

So let's forget about societal norms and shame,
It's just us two here, no need for playing games.
Give me all of you, your dick and your touch,
And I'll moan and writhe as you make my pussy clutch.

~

No need to be silent or hold back that lust,
Let's embrace our desires with passion and trust.
Together we'll explore new heights of ecstasy,
Because in this realm of pleasure, it's just you and me.

Sexvation

Time: 23:45

Date: 27.10.2015

Open your legs, my love, spread them wide,
Let me indulge in your pleasure, take you on a wild ride.
I'll take care of your desires, satisfy your every need,
In this intimate dance, our passions will exceed.

~

Feel my tongue explore, as I kiss and caress,
Your moans of delight, they simply confess.
Your pussy, a treasure I'm eager to adore,
Together we'll reach heights like never before.

~

No need for translation, our bodies speak the same,
In this erotic symphony, there's no room for shame.
You've unleashed a fire within me that can't be contained,
So let go of all inhibitions and let pleasure reign.

~

It's not your fault for being so incredibly alluring,
Our connection electrifying, endlessly enduring.
Scream out your ecstasy, let it fill the air,
As we lose ourselves in passion without a care.

~

Your hands are moving,
And I think that's a sign of demonstration,

But let's switch gears and engage in some oral stimulation,
It's time to explore each other's desires with dedication,
Hmm, tonight we'll indulge in some passionate sensation.

~

I'm not just talking about the physical satisfaction,

But also the emotional connection and mental elevation,
Together we'll create a symphony of pleasure and elation,
As we navigate the depths of our intimate exploration.

The Orgasmic Cure for Stress

Time: 02:48
Date: 28.10.2015

Let's just fuck in the pouring rain,
Where stress washes away, no need to explain,
As the government takes every grain,
We'll embrace the pleasure and forget the strain.

~

Fuck me with passion, release my pent-up desires,
In this stormy weather, let's light our own fires,
Kissing in the rain, our bodies entwined,
Making love under dark clouds, leaving all worries behind.

~

Feel the drops on our skin, like nature's sweet caress,
Finding bliss in each other's arms, no need to suppress,
No swear words needed, just love and connection,
In this wet embrace, finding pure satisfaction.

~

When the rain subsides and clears from sight,
Our memories of this moment will forever ignite,
And as the water drains away with a gentle flow,
We'll cherish the intimacy we shared, both high and low.

~

My frustration is melting,
Quickly bind me with the chain,
Let's indulge in passion,
Make me lose my sane.
Oh how I loathed existence,

But now your love is my cocaine.

~

You're erasing all my worries,
Yes, your touch is what I've gained.
Now, let's stroll to the car,
And light up a joint of Mary Jane.
Drive to the airport,
Fly away to Spain.

~

Once we land on foreign soil,
Unpack our bags with glee,
Then, make fuck once more,
In wild ecstasy.

~

Oh yes,
Relief from stress,
Let's sip some champagne, and have more sex.

Hunger for Healing
Time: 03:51
Date: 28.10.2015

Your incapabilities should not hinder your performance in bed, So let's continue on, no need to dread.

~

I crave for you to caress me with your lips,
Bringing pleasure as our bodies intertwine and hips sway, never miss.

~

Explore every inch of me with tender care,
Leaving no spot untouched, no desire left to spare.

~

Forget about using your hands, let your tongue be the guide,
As we indulge in the passionate dance of oral delight.
No need for eye contact, just focus on the sensations we share, For tonight, it's all about pleasure without any strings or love affair.

~

In this moment, all I desire is your touch and embrace,
A temporary escape from reality, a euphoric space.

~

Avoid looking into my eyes, for tears may start to flow,
I don't want you falling in love, I'm not ready to let go.

~

In this moment, all I crave is your touch and affection,
Let's lose ourselves in the ecstasy of our connection.

~

So let go of inhibitions, surrender to the ecstasy we create,
For tonight, it's about pure satisfaction and fulfilling our fate.

Orgasmic Odyssey

Time: 03:32

Date: 28.10.2015

Let's not depart, without exploring the art of lovemaking,
Let's embrace passion's fire, our bodies vibrating.

~

We can indulge in the ecstasy of an oceanfront tryst,
As the waves crash beside us, our desires persist.

~

In a secluded suite, we'll explore every inch,
With whispered moans and gasps, our bodies will flinch.

~

If curious eyes wander, we'll quickly hide in shame,
Our secret rendezvous protected from any blame.

~

Making love under the stars, our bodies entwined,
Caressing and kissing, a euphoric state of mind.

~

Upon the bedroom floor, we'll create our own symphony,
Lost in pleasure's rhythm, a sensuous melody.

~

Let's slip into attire and venture to the night's scene,
Dancing and laughing, like nothing we've ever seen.

~

So let us not pass by this chance to explore,
Lets fuck all night, then take up our clothing from the floor.

Until it's my time, I will write.
With love,
Chavanese Wint

www.ingramcontent.com/pod-product-compliance
Lightning Source LLC
Chambersburg PA
CBHW051831160426
43209CB00006B/1119